DAYS OUT
IN DORSET

Written and illustrated by

JOY PARSONS

© Joy Parsons 2002
ISBN 1 897 887 30 2

This edition (3rd) published by:
Natula Publications
Natula, 5 St Margarets Avenue, Christchurch, Dorset BH23 1JD
E-Mail: info@natula.co.uk

First published by Thornhill Press 1981
ISBN 0 904 110 90 1

Printed by Impress Print, Corby, Northamptonshire NN18 8EW

Details are accurate at the time of publication but may be liable to change. For up-to-date information of opening times, admission prices, special events, wheelchair and pushchair access to the attractions please enquire at Tourist Information Centres or contact the attractions directly. A list of web sites can be found at the back of this book.

The publishers would like to thank all the organisations that kindly provided and confirmed the accuracy of information included in this book.

Front Cover Illustrations:
Main Picture: Corfe Castle
Inset: Squirrel Monkey, Monkey World

CONTENTS

CONTENTS (Continued)

INTRODUCTION

It seems incredible to me that 21 years have melted away since this little book first surfaced and sold out, was reprinted and sold out again. Then, for some reason it disappeared from my horizon and memory. It has now been suggested to me that it should reappear and so with the help of my publisher, here it is again, refurbished and enlarged to act as a courier from the Dorset countryside.

Stair Hole
Lulworth Cove

So many changes have occurred in the world – some better, some undoubtedly worse. In December 2001, however, the spectacular Dorset and East Devon coastline acquired World Heritage status – England's first Natural World Heritage making the Jurassic coast equivalent to the USA's Grand Canyon and Australia's Great Barrier Reef. The coast records 185 million years of the Earth's history through the Triassic, Jurassic and Cretaceous periods of geological time. It also has outstanding examples of geomorphology such as **Durdle Door**. Of the 46 known species of Jurassic fish, 35 of them are only found on the Dorset and East Devon coast.

Famous people like Thomas Hardy, Jane Austen, J.M. Turner, John Constable and John Fowles have all been stimulated by the Dorset magic of which I am always newly aware each time I revisit one of these places.

As the idea of beauty lies in the beholder, all this book can do is to act as a signpost and leave you, the traveller, to form your own impressions and nostalgias for a particular place. Every county has its own type of charm and the works of Thomas Hardy certainly enhance but are not the origin of this special magic they merely add a fillip to a day's outing, be it a corner of old Poole, an outlying hamlet, a trip to Portland to gaze upon and wonder at **Chesil Beach** or a wander and a wonderment amongst the rolling hills. Within the boundaries every taste is catered for: artists, historians and archaeologists, ornithologists, children wanting sea, sandy beaches and amusements or folk in search of rural retreat. It matters not the starting point or the season; when the golden corn is glowing in the summer sun or when the hedgerows are sparkling with hoar frost and the blackbirds showing up starkly in a temporary fairyland. As life is made up of strong contrasts so it is with Dorset, from the harsh and jagged coast of **St Aldhelm's Head** to the delicacy of the Chalk Hill Butterfly.

The ideal thing, of course, is to explore on foot but in this age of the car most of the spots I pinpoint are accessible or nearly so, by this means. The nooks and crannies you will find for yourself so once again I wish you 'Happy Days Out'.

CHRISTCHURCH

Once part of Hampshire, the ancient town of Christchurch is now part of Dorset. Christchurch inhabitants are indeed lucky and it is easy to see why folk keep moving down here from the cold north. We certainly get the best of the weather combined with such contrasting, accessible beauty spots – the New Forest on one side and the coastline and Purbecks on the other. The magnificent Priory Church dominates the scene and is really best viewed from

Christchurch Priory from the East

across the estuary from **Hengistbury Head**, which in itself, reeks of ancient history. It has the longest nave of any parish church in England and has been standing on this spot for 9 centuries. It is a source of admiration and wonderment for the steady flow of visitors. The church was dedicated to the Holy Trinity and the town was originally known as Twynham. Many people will not have realised that both acquired the name Christchurch on account of the belief in the amazing story of the Miraculous Beam which having been accidentally cut too short during building operations, was not only lengthened but also placed in its correct position overnight without human aid. Spiritual intervention also determined that the Priory should be built on its present site instead of on top of St. Catherine's Hill as originally planned; the foundation materials were all transported mysteriously overnight to the banks of the Avon from the top of the hill. So there it was erected aided by an unknown workman who never drew any pay or took refreshment and who disappeared upon completion leaving behind the belief that he was none other than Christ himself.

Christchurch Harbour with its narrow mouth, locally known as The Run, is picturesque but very treacherous to would-be sailors as the channel is always changing its course. The quay at **Mudeford** offers many aesthetic moments and for me one of them is the amazing number of starlings and sparrows that flock around the lobster pots and visitor's parked cars in search

of pickings and even eyeing the plates on the tables outside the well-known Haven Inn! There is a popular fresh-fish stall on the quay. Although much coastal defence work has been done in this area you can still wander around the old Dutch Houses and Lifeboat Station or sit and watch the sun going down behind the Priory silhouette in the evening – I have done much sketching from this spot!

Hengistbury Head with its considerable archaeological history, its wildlife, beach and café can be reached by ferry across 'The Run' from Mudeford Quay. It can also be approached from western end by car or bus and then by the delightful 'Noddy Train' with its little open carriages to the colourful row of beach huts on the sand spit enclosing the harbour.

In the town centre at 11 o'clock on Monday mornings during the summer months the Town Crier, in all his traditional finery, conducts a tour around the town. To add to the colourful scene the local weekly market is held in the High Street on a Monday.

The town tour may well take you past the captivating Red House Museum and Art Gallery (not open on Mondays) where in summer the Museum garden with its lily pond, old-fashioned rose trees and herb garden make a restful refuge amidst the town's business and trade. In the entrance foyer you will probably be surprised by the unusual and wide range of collectible items that are for sale – just to mention some of them: hand-crafted jewellery and doll's house furniture, crystals and wild flower seeds, herbal oils and attractive glassware items, replicas of fascinating footwear, minerals and fossils but the two things that caught

my eye specially were the small really old-fashioned slates and little pots of 'Too many Strawberries' jam! There is also a frequently varying selection of greetings cards. Refreshments in the form of tea, coffee and hot chocolate are available in the area where there is a good selection of books and booklets on sale.

The quay close to the Priory precincts can provide many an hour's idling, aided if necessary by a picnic on the grass or a visit to a nearby café, restaurant or old smuggling inn. During the summer months there is a regular

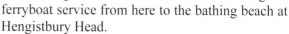

ferryboat service from here to the bathing beach at Hengistbury Head.

Convent Walk alongside the Mill Stream and in the shadow of the Priory and castle ruins is a favourite haunt. Approached from the quayside it opens out at the Town Bridge where you may be lucky enough to see fishermen in the boat landing a sea trout. The hosts of mallards and swans here on the River Avon are a great attraction.

Another point of interest is Ducking Stool Lane where a replica ducking stool was installed in 1986 and was also used as a result of the Court Leet having been reintroduced and having sat in the town for the first time since 1937. The Court Leet was the main judicial and local government court and it met in the old building that now accommodates the New Forest Perfumery and cafe. Dating back to medieval days or earlier, apparently several hundred Court Leets still operate in the country but no longer have legal powers and are mostly ceremonial and highly entertaining.

HIGHCLIFFE CASTLE

Built between 1830 and 1835 by Sir Charles Stuart, later to become Lord Stuart de Rothesay, this handsome Grade I building in its beautiful setting has much to offer. It is also of much interest internationally on account of having medieval French masonry incorporated into its structure, in particular a notable oriel window. Now having been restored from its previous dereliction by the combined efforts of the local council, English Heritage and a grant from the Heritage Lottery Fund, it has given a new venue to the local people and visitors alike. It is actually the second house to be built on this site. The original house, built by Lord Stuart de Rothesay's grandfather, was called High Cliff.

The Castle history and that of previous owners is tastefully displayed on an interior wall. Various exhibitions take place therein and it is licensed for civil wedding ceremonies and, not surprisingly, is becoming increasingly popular for this purpose.

My first visit as I wandered and 'took stock' of it all was drawn to a glimpse through a mass of rhododendrons of a corner of the building (always attracted by a 'flowery' angle, this is what I remembered) and later in the season the literal forest of foxgloves (Fairy Gloves, Elfin Caps, Digitalis – take your pick) which you pass on the walk to the cliff and beach.

However, back to the less aesthetic – there is a pleasant café that is open all year round and a well and interestingly stocked shop. The Castle is closed during January and February. There is, of course, a magnificent view of Bournemouth Bay and the Isle of Wight from the cliff top.

Do you believe in fairies? It is not difficult, wandering alone here on the cliff top on a cold grey day, I must say. I felt bewitched by the primeval looking tree silhouettes – their foliage swaying and bending over my head in the gale force wind, a weird and wonderful entwinement of branches, many reaching out over the cliff edge. I felt I <u>must</u> get an impression of them – huge Holm oaks and mighty pines. Undoubtedly faerie habitat! The 'Oak Men' or 'Brownies' are the tree spirits according to a book by Brian Froud and Alan Lee, and they can be dangerous if their tree is cut down, so beware of further pruning!

St Marks Church, which was consecrated in 1843, was built on land donated by Lord Stuart de Rothesay from the considerable estate. Lord and Lady Stuart de Rothesay brought the church bell back from Russia during their travels.

BOURNEMOUTH

This well-known holiday resort with its pine trees, attractive Chines and magnificent sandy beach which continues as far as Sandbanks on one side and Hengistbury Head on the other, really needs little publicity. It has, of course, all the usual amenities for the holiday-maker including piers, concert halls, cinemas, night clubs, many good shops, museums and various activities for youngsters. Windsurfing and board surfing flourish here and there are many other water sports on offer along this part of the coastline.

Aesthetically the Upper and Lower Gardens are a delight, with the little silver Bourne stream gurgling through them. The resident grey squirrel population is thriving, unfortunately at the expense of local birds, and many are quite tame. They are fed by a surprising number of people who appear daily with bags of nuts for them. There is an aviary in the Lower Gardens and during the summer there is an open-air art gallery here too. The Russell Cotes Art Gallery and Museum perched high on the East Cliff top is worth a visit (not open on Mondays) and many treasures and pleasures are to be found therein, including a new interactive Children's Gallery.

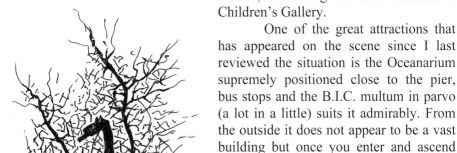

One of the great attractions that has appeared on the scene since I last reviewed the situation is the Oceanarium supremely positioned close to the pier, bus stops and the B.I.C. multum in parvo (a lot in a little) suits it admirably. From the outside it does not appear to be a vast building but once you enter and ascend the curving staircase you wander through an apparently large area of turns and twists with fish of every variety swimming around. The cleverly arranged aquariums enable you to see the fish from above, below and sideways. There is also an underwater tunnel.

One of the two main objects of my visit was to see the two green sea turtles (Crusoe and Friday). They were originally washed up in Cornwall before being transferred to Bournemouth. Apparently turtles navigate by the sun and stars but lose their way if it becomes cloudy! They can reach the age of 200 years and are the longest living invertebrates. They can stay underwater for a long time without air and are often seen resting on the bottom of the aquarium, so don't imagine that they are ill.

My next target were the sea horses – charming little creatures. I finally spotted several, one apparently very young and pale showing up well against the dark, lacy pattern of the coral to which he hung by his prehensile tail. While I was there I managed a quick drawing of the head of the tiger fish and I shall undoubtedly go again to draw the iguana.

ALDERHOLT MILL

This picturesque mill standing as it does on the Dorset-Hampshire border offers a most enjoyable outing. It is a particularly pleasant spot with its rippling trout stream in front and the big wheel and pool at the rear. The present owners have fully restored it and now it is once again a working mill. The machinery can be seen working and there are milling demonstrations on Sunday afternoons. The former craft centre now accommodates holiday homes whilst the main mill house offers B&B facilities, cream teas are also available.

Water vole

Alderholt is thought to be an outlying hamlet of Cranborne Manor and takes its name from the surrounding alder trees and the fact that the river here used to be frequented by otters. During the medieval period the customary tenants of the village were obliged to have their grain ground here as one of the customs of the Manor.

CRANBORNE

The River Crane flowing through Cranborne adds to the attraction of this little town. It is strange how the guidebook opinions about Cranborne vary; some dismiss it, others uphold it; I find it seductive. Approaching it from the Verwood road takes you past the hamlet of **Edmonsham** with its setback, nestling church. It may be of interest to see the quantity of mistletoe growing in so many of the surrounding trees. (Mistletoe used to be cut from the oak trees by the Druids, with a golden knife, for their religious rites.) Edmonsham House and gardens are open to the public and well worth a visit.

In Springtime Cranborne Church, which is one of the largest in the country (141 feet long), is made magical by the surrounding daffodils and the lovely heartening cawing from the rookery nearby. It was built in 1252 and is situated on the foundations of a monastery. It contains considerable traces of 13th century frescoes that must once have been magnificent. Like so many other Dorset churches this church has been restored by previous generations and these frescoes only came to light again in 1898. The font has seen 700 years service.

Medieval Cranborne was an important Dorset town and the elegant and chiefly Tudor Manor House has seen many noble and royal visitors and is quite one of the most attractive stately homes. The imposing drive through a long avenue of beech trees takes you through an archway with two little gatehouses into the enclosed courtyard in front of the Manor. When I visited the Manor in May (please note: the house is not open to the public) it was enchanting and contained a delightful 'white garden' where all the flowers were white and had a vista from the loggia down through a line on either side of bent and gnarled apple trees, some of which were over 100 years old and still bearing fruit. The garden was originally laid out in the 17th century and today's dedicated gardeners help create an impression of alternate patches of intentional untended charm and well-kept sophistication. Colour greeted me on every side and each vivid tulip appeared to be of a different variety. A special corner to me was the loggia on which there were 2 tubs each with a splendid white rhododendron that had grown to fine proportions and peeped out over the parapet in an endearing way.

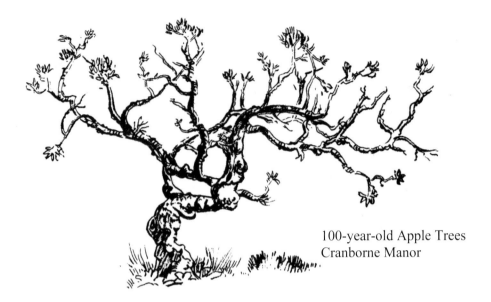

100-year-old Apple Trees
Cranborne Manor

The rear entrance to the Manor, through its avenue of trees leading off Swan Street that is in fact a small square, is just as imposing as the front elevation. It now boasts a modern Manor Gardens Centre with grey statuary and clipped yew hedges.

Down the road is the old Fleur de Lys Inn, which Hardy mentioned in *Tess of the d'Urbervilles* and is well worth visiting before, perhaps, you continue a few miles further to inspect the villages of the Gussage Valley. You make the acquaintance of **Gussage All Saints** by way of a sharp right-hand turn marked up in large letters as 'Ahmen Corner' which has the desired effect of pulling one up sharp. The church in this medieval village has three bells reputedly older than the Reformation and the village is known to have been built on the site of an Iron Age chariot factory.

On to **Gussage St. Michael** which also has an ancient church and a fantastically large yew tree. If you wish to search further along the valley there is also **Gussage St. Andrew**. The 12th century church here has some notable medieval wall paintings.

In this sequestered area you get the feeling that nobody ever hurries – and what a relief it is!

WIMBORNE SAINT GILES

Wimborne St. Giles becomes firmly entrenched in the mind. It is truly a Dorset gem. St. Giles House, which is unfortunately not open to the public, sits in its 400-acre park and has been the home of the Earls of Shaftesbury since c.1650. Particularly noteworthy are the many reforms and beneficent Acts secured by the efforts of the 7th Earl of Shaftesbury. Responsible for the abolition of much child labour, he recounted the conditions under which they worked in the mines, the factories and in the sweeping of chimneys, the reading of which emphasises its marked contrast to today when every worker is so conscious of his rights. It must surely have been his untiring efforts to expose and oppose that were the source of the aura of peace and gentleness that still envelopes this tucked-away village with its interesting church and 300-year-old almshouse. The statue, Eros, in Piccadilly Circus in London is a memorial to him. It is said that the arrow Eros is holding points directly to St. Giles House.

Not far from the church the River Allen meanders by and an item of interest on the roadside is the renewed village stocks, now protected by a cedar tiled roof and surrounded by railings. Not far behind this relic is a mass of ancient apple trees festooned with lacy, delicate lichen: subtle colours and patterns that become even more interesting to a painter on a wet day.

On entering the church the visitor is somewhat surprised by the glitter of gold from the ornate cover to the font which faces the door. Dating from 1752 it was given by the 9th Earl of Shaftesbury in memory of his sisters Evelyn Baring, Violet Mar and Kellie.

It is an interesting thought that the first cabbage grown in England was raised, so it is said, here in this village by Sir Anthony Ashley of St. Giles House. He was an enthusiastic gardener and the strange ball on his tomb in the Lady Chapel bears a close resemblance to this time-honoured vegetable!

WIMBORNE MINSTER

 Here is a town whose life, quite rightly, revolves around and is justly proud of its splendid Minster with its two towers and noticeably colourful stonework. This is worth observing after a shower of rain or on a wet day when all nature's pigments become twice as powerful to the human eye. Quite apart from the many interesting tombs (including a brass in the paving stones indicating the grave of King Ethelred beneath it), the unique chained library dating from 1686 and the celebrated Saxon oak chest, the real showpiece is inside on the wall of the Western Tower. It is the incredible Astronomical Clock. With a dial dating from the 14th or 15th century it is a truly fantastic piece of machinery and was restored last century at a great cost. Attached to the clock and outside a window in this tower perched up high and chiming away each fifteen minutes of life by means of the tools he holds in his hands is the wooden and brightly painted figure of 'Quarter Jack'. His name is self-explanatory and he provides a certain focal point for the tourists who inundate the town each summer.

The Priests House Museum is well worth visiting and is right in the centre of the town. Housed in a 16th century Grade II listed building it contains an extremely interesting collection of objects and displays covering the archaeology and local history of East Dorset. It also has a truly delightful walled garden that reaches right back to the pretty River Allen. The garden with its 300-year-old wisteria is a tranquil haven in this busy little town.

It would be a great mistake in this age of 'expendables', plastic and quick fix commodities not to visit Walford Mill Craft Centre. Situated on a little island amongst peaceful grounds through which you can stroll, it is an ideal site for a working craft centre. Inside the tastefully renovated 18th century building are the workshops and a shop that sells a truly uplifting display of handcrafted delights. On the day of my last visit there was an exhibition of Master Glass in the light and airy gallery – fragile and beautiful. Moving on past the silver jewellery and ceramics of all descriptions, myriads of greetings cards – you can have your own unique one made on the spot – and up to the next floor you can watch the silk weaver at work. If by now you feel in need of refreshment there is a bistro happily situated in the grounds of the Mill.

Wimborne Minster
from Corfe Mullen

Despite the fact that my visit happened to be on a grey, wet day I came away with raised spirits having had the sight and recognition of so much genuine talent still flourishing in Dorset.

Another rewarding afternoon can be spent in Deans Court Garden, right in the centre of this bustling town if you can make it on one of the few days it is open to the public each year. (Contact the Wimborne Tourist Information Centre for further details.) It is so utterly peaceful with its 13 acres of partly wild garden on the River Allen. A monastery fishpond, unusual trees and herb garden make for enjoyment whilst the peacocks add great elegance to the scene.

The Model Village that provides a genuine reflection of what the town was like in the 1950s and the large bustling market held on Fridays, Saturdays and Sundays are also worth visiting while you are in Wimborne. The market is one of the largest in the south of England and a vast range of goods can be found on the stalls jostling for attention in the covered bazaar and in the overspill outside. On Fridays collectors can be seen avidly scrutinising the antique and bric-a-brac stalls.

If, whilst in the district, you are drawn to the village of **Sturminster Marshall,** perhaps to visit the White Mill (National Trust), take time to look at the two village greens. One is home to the old stocks and the other has an impressive maypole. Give your imagination full rein to conjure up the mental visions of the colour, movement and gaiety which occurres as the ancient fertility symbolic dance is carried out around the maypole on May Day each year.

As a contrast, the medieval bridge crossing the River Stour nearby and which can be approached from the turning off the Wimborne-Blandford Road evokes an atmosphere of stillness, peace and beauty. From this viewpoint the church on its Norman foundations shows itself from afar. It has, like all Dorset places of worship, many items within to inspect and remark upon, including an ancient helmet which apparently belonged to the Churchill family. For those who wish, there is much to be researched historically. For instance, Thomas Merke, the brave Bishop of Carlisle, after all his daring speeches and friendship with Richard II, came in the latter years of his life to preach here to his few parishioners.

Shapwick, a neighbouring village which got its name meaning 'sheep village' in Saxon times, lies close beside the River Stour and takes you onto the Wimborne-Blandford road once again – a nice little detour. The road here is uniquely lined on each side by magnificent beech trees. I think this is one of the loveliest parts of Dorset. Crossing it directly **Badbury Rings**, the great Iron Age hill fort (now owned by the National Trust and part of the Kingston Lacy Estate), can be reached. Quite apart from its legends and history this is a superb viewpoint on a suitable day. It is always a pleasant place to visit, enhanced to my mind by the tradition that King Arthur's soul inhabited the body of a nesting raven at this spot. It is also supposed to be one of the last nesting places of this mysterious, remote bird.

KNOLL GARDENS

Variegated and exotic ornamental grasses seem to be the vogue these days, and where better to find a type to suit your personal taste than at Knoll Gardens, Hampreston, where these plants are their speciality. There are now so many garden centres around the countryside to choose from that it is refreshing to find one that concentrates on something a little different.

The other item that particularly attracts me here is the Dragon guarding the Koi carp pool. In reality these dragons are members of the lizard family (Australia has a flying variety). Mythically they are portrayed as being adept with tooth and claw and spitting fire! This one, however, is a sculpture based on St. Dunstan, one of four Saints of Wessex depicted in a stained glass window in Wimborne Minster. It was commissioned in 1991 and sculpted by Susan Ford.

EAST DORSET

A354

A338

• GUSSAGE ST ANDREW

◈ CRANBORNE

WIMBORNE ST GILES

• FORDINGBRIDGE

◈ ALDERHOLT

GUSSAGE •
ST MICHAEL

• GUSSAGE
ALL SAINTS

• EDMONSHAM

• VERWOOD

A31

• RINGWOOD

• BADBURY RINGS

• MOORS VALLEY
COUNTRY PARK

SHAPWICK

◈ KINGSTON LACY

A31

STAPEHILL ◈

A338

• STURMINSTER
MARSHALL

◈ KNOLL GARDENS

◈ WIMBORNE

A348

• BOURNEMOUTH
INT AIRPORT

A35

TOWER PARK •

A35

UPTON ◈
COUNTRY PARK

CHRISTCHURCH ◈

HIGHCLIFF
CASTLE ◈

◈ MUDEFORD

Poole
Harbour

◈ POOLE

BOURNEMOUTH ◈

Hengistbury
Head

BROWNSEA ISLAND ◈

Sandbanks

◈ LOCATIONS WITH FEATURED CHAPTERS

Studland

20

St. Dunstan is the patron saint of goldsmiths and craftsmen and his emblem is a harp. Legend has it that the Devil tried to tempt St. Dunstan as he worked and when the Devil's gossiping became too much St. Dunstan struck him on the nose with his hot tongs and as you will see the sculpture is so arranged that St. Dunstan becomes part of the harp and the dragon the Devil.

'Wimborne Botanic' as it was known 30 years ago began with some Australasian plants and a collection of rhododendrons. A gravel garden with sun-loving plants that tolerate drought conditions has recently been added and another of the gardens has been planted specifically for dry but shady areas.

The Dorset Wildlife Trust and Knoll Gardens have been working together to find ways in which horticulture and wildlife can thrive side-by-side. There is free access to Knoll Gardens (from March to October inclusive) for R.H.S. members and free entry to the visitor centre, nursery and licensed coffee shop for visitors.

KINGSTON LACY

There are many impressive and beautiful country houses available to the public for viewing but in the grounds of the 17th century house of Kingston

Lacy I feel there is something quite magical – after a long dark winter to go there in the spring and to get the visual impact of the veritable snowdrop carpet extending in all directions is, for me anyway, an experience of pure delight – an uplift of the spirit after the struggles of winter. (The grounds are not usually open during the months November to March so telephone Kingston Lacy direct for details of these special dates.) The estate extends to 250 acres of wooded parkland that is home to a herd of splendid Red Devon Cattle.

Kingston Lacy House, designed by Roger Pratt for the Bankes family and bequeathed to the National Trust in 1981, contains a remarkable collection of paintings including works by Van Dyck, Titian and Breughel. Amongst the fine collection of Egyptian artefacts there are exhibits dating from 3000BC including sarcophagi and an obelisk or 'Cleopatra's Needle' set in the landscaped gardens. There is also a shop, a restaurant and a play trail for children. The house is open daily (except Mondays and Tuesdays) from April to October inclusive.

STAPEHILL

WARNING! Stapehill is really an 'all-day job' – there is so much to see that the odd hour goes nowhere. To begin there is ample parking and the actual entrance to the building is unusual for a start. Once you have passed through it there is a sense of pleasurable mystery. You will be provided with an exploratory map but I declined to look at mine and preferred to just wander at first. The active water wheel greets you as you head for the exhibition of 'Power to the Land' that consists of all the old agricultural and horticultural equipment you can think of. The first item that caught my eye was the picture of the first basic tractor, which came from America (the Froleich, 1892). It had an exposed engine and only 15-20 horsepower. Compare this to the gleaming and active traction engine, the Earl of Eldon (originally from Corfe Castle), which takes its place in the annual Steam Rally held in June.

The smell and atmosphere are remarkably realistic as one wanders on past the farrier figure with his equipment, the village chemist's shop, and the old scarecrow complete with straw hat (seldom seen nowadays as mechanical scarers are used instead). Nostalgic portrayal of people haymaking in the pre-mechanised days of the old scythe and sickle; old milk churns in the farm delivery cart with the pint measure alongside and cheese making urns were reminiscent of my childhood days when I used to play on a friend's farm and sneak into the 'operation quarters' where we were allowed to eat a bite or two of the curd.

After this you may be drawn to the farmyard where you will be met by a mixed flock of extremely free and happy hens, enquiring geese, guinea fowl and ducks. There are also goats, sheep and cows to be seen and really fresh eggs to buy.

Until 1900 there were more than 100 Trappist nuns in the Abbey but few young women since then have been prepared to take up the strict and silent life. Eventually the remaining little group moved to Whitland in Dyfed, S.W. Wales. Now the Abbey with its renovated buildings and surroundings still retains its ambience and gives pleasure to an ever-increasing number of visitors.

As you approach the Cistine Chapel a gentle chanting will be heard and further exploration will show you the original Mother Superior's seat and that of the Abbess and deputy Abbess alongside the well-worn piece of flooring still remaining. You can read about the history of Stapehill from the notice hanging on the wall by the ancient steps leading to the Chapel.

You can rest awhile in the cloister garden before moving on past the tropical greenhouse with its steamy atmosphere reminiscent of rain forests to Stapehill's millennium effort – the truly beautiful Japanese Garden with its shrines, bamboo and waterfalls. You can venture up the steps to the viewpoint and then surprising and pleasant at any time but on my visiting day, with the autumn sun glittering across the water and extremely tame ducks and moorhens (and a black swan) crowding around the lake, it was a superb end to my day out!

There is so much to see that I had concentrated mainly on the ground level but on the upper floors there were crafts on display, many being demonstrated too.

POOLE

Poole will enchant you by its diversity of interests: scenic, recreational and historical. Its beautiful inland harbour, the largest in Europe, with its islands, inlets and hidden peaceful corners is virtually unchanged since the days when it was a smuggler's paradise. Its busy quay with numerous trips available for sightseeing or fishing makes it a delight for all ages. Probably the best impression of the lovely harbour can be seen from Constitution Hill, Parkstone, where a whole range of atmospheric effects can be viewed, if necessary from a car.

As a painter I am particularly drawn to the area of Poole Quay beside the old lifeboat station (now the Lifeboat Museum). Here you can enjoy the little inner harbour, the small craft and above all the fishing nets drying on their lines. Nowadays the supporting poles are of steel instead of old timber and the floats polystyrene instead of cork, but nevertheless it is still very picturesque.

Back towards the High Street and the Old Town you pass by the famous Poole Pottery shop and retail outlet near the new Marina Complex on the quay. Two museums, the Waterfront and Scaplen's Court (once the old Guildhall) are situated close to each other near the quay. Scaplen's Court is only open during August whereas the Waterfront Museum is open all year round. The Parish Church of St. James, also in the Old Town, has a beautiful Georgian interior and unique pillars that resemble ship's masts.

Between the vast shopping complex and Sandbanks, Poole Park will give long hours of enjoyment, especially to bird watchers. Here Canada geese, tufted ducks, gulls, oystercatchers, mallards and pigeons wander across the grass and wait to be fed by passers-by. The silhouette of the cormorants on posts with wings outstretched and drying in the sun is a familiar one. My last visit during Christmas week in a fierce gale was the most rewarding ever: there must have been literally hundreds of tufted ducks on the smaller lake in front of the well-placed restaurant while at its rear about 50 Canada geese were parading on the grass. A lone visitor with a bag of bread became practically invisible amongst the swooping, shrieking flock of gulls.

Next to the restaurant is an indoor adventure playground for youngsters. Other activities on offer include a miniature railway, boat hire and windsurfing. (Further out of the town centre to the north the large Tower Park Leisure Complex offers a wealth of indoor activities including Splashdown - a water park with lots of slides and rides.)

Leaving the park, perhaps reluctantly, and then proceeding along Shore Road with the ferry and **Studland** in mind, it will pay you to deviate slightly and visit the superb gardens of Compton Acres at Canford Cliffs. To my mind spring is the best time to go as the azaleas are ablaze with colour. A new deer sanctuary, spectacular views over Poole Harbour and the Purbeck Hills and a large restaurant amongst the tall pine trees all add to an enjoyable outing. There are many different, formally laid out gardens to see: Japanese, Roman, Indian, Spanish, and Italian to name but some and the new Sensory Sculpture Garden with its highly scented plants and shrubs growing in between variously textured stone sculptures is an out of the ordinary experience. Compton Acres is open from March until the end of October.

BROWNSEA ISLAND

Brownsea is the largest of the islands in Poole Harbour and extends over 500 acres. Now owned by the National Trust it is a happy place to spend a day. From April to mid October boats ply daily at frequent intervals from the ferry side at Sandbanks and Poole Quay transporting visitors to land at the Town Quay. There is a landing fee to be paid but it is free to National Trust members. Please note that no dogs other than guide dogs are allowed on the island. Part of the island is a nature reserve run by the Wildlife Trust and a daily tour (starting at 2pm) is well worth doing.

Henry VIII is said to have been responsible for the original castle that he began as a square blockhouse to protect Poole and he appointed 6 men for 'keeping the watch'. This building in due course became a castle with a tower and barbican. It was almost completely burnt down in 1896 but was rebuilt the following year and now forms a point of interest at the mouth of the harbour. It was also on this island that Lord Baden Powell founded the Boy Scout movement.

Tranquillity is the operative word here. You can walk to obtain splendid views from the high vantage points, enjoy the daffodil field ablaze in April (a relic of a flower growing venture some time back), seek out the quaint beaches, enjoy bird watching from the observation hut, stroll in the sunshine on Peacock Hill whereupon is perched the church or perhaps go to the church service on a Sunday (3pm throughout the season). There are 2 shops, one National Trust and the other supplying sweets and ice cream. There is also a refreshment room.

Here, such a surprisingly short distance from the mainland amongst the calling peacocks which roam at will, the glimpses of golden pheasants or red squirrels, you can really feel away from it all.

UPTON COUNTRY PARK

Situated on the south side of the A35/A3049 crossroads and about 4 miles from the centre of the ever-encroaching urban sprawl of Poole lies Upton Country Park.

The Upton Estate came into the hands of a wealthy merchant, Christopher Spurrier, who, trading between Poole and Newfoundland had amassed a fortune. He built Upton House, which is now a Grade II listed building, in 1818. The house, which has been added to over the years, is of

special architectural interest: on the outside of the building the unusual curving colonnaded screens on either side of the main block and inside, the Adam-style ceilings and the hall, decorated in black marble and Portland stone rising to the full height of the building gives it a somewhat dramatic effect.

There is much attractive variation within the 100-acre grounds, which can be viewed by following the nature trails. There are pleasant views of Poole Harbour from the terraces and the front field is ideal for hiring for special events. The walled garden with its long, wide and colourful border is a source of much pleasure and I was particularly struck by the big wrought iron gate at the end with its little fish motive. The Peacock Tearooms are open 7 days a week.

WAREHAM

The quay where the Old Granary Restaurant is happily situated beside the River Frome, has in ancient days known the export of clay and the import of coal and other commodities. Wareham, from being a busy and vital port in days past, has now become a pause for tourists in Dorset, inviting them to rest awhile in its rather peaceful atmosphere, to explore its back streets and markets and wander by the peaceful rivers.

Wareham has various churches, one of which is now a tourist information and heritage centre, but the most unusual, perhaps, is St Martin-on-the-Walls at the north entrance to the town. It is thought to have been founded by St. Aldhelm in 698. Here within its historic walls you can see medieval wall paintings and find a stone effigy of Lawrence of Arabia, dressed in the flowing robes of an Arab, which was presented by his brother. Lawrence of Arabia was buried a short distance away at **Moreton**. You can visit his tiny cottage at **Clouds Hill**, which he bought in 1925 as a retreat and is now owned by the National Trust. The cottage and grounds are open between April and October but are closed on Mondays, Tuesdays and Wednesdays. A commemorative stone marks the scene of his tragic road accident on one of the lonely roads across the heath, nearby, where he met his death. The Tank Museum at **Bovington** also has a special 'Lawrence Feature' including a description of his RAF service. There is also the Lawrence of Arabia Trail beginning at the Tank Museum, where parking and refreshments are available, and visiting the sites concerned with his life in this part of Dorset passing en route beautiful countryside.

Undoubtedly, gentle Wareham has a great deal to show those who will search out its North, South, East and West Streets which were so painstakingly set up by the Romans on the points of the compass.

CORFE

It is not known exactly when the first castle was built here. In 978, when King Edward was murdered at the instigation of his stepmother, this site was fortified. We do know that the first stones of this imposing and well-known castle were laid down in 1076 and that the reign of Stephen produced its first siege. Its blood-curdling history of imprisonments for those who wish to search them out will produce a spinal shiver even on a hot summer's day. So magnificently built and perched high on the hill it is almost unbelievable that once in later years it somehow withstood the blast resulting from a Parliamentary order to blow it up. Such was the British workmanship in days gone by ….

The village is charming; its mellow stonework displays the wondrous variety of the greys to be found in English skies. It wanders in three directions and has a name for cream teas in the cafes around its market place and in hidden corners. It offers for your observance the church containing amongst other items of interest a 15th century font made from local marble, the Town House with its stone roof and a traditional little museum (free entry) containing examples of iguanodon-type dinosaur's footprints which contrast rather sharply with a few 'props' from the comparatively recent filming in this area of *The Mayor of Casterbridge.*

THE BLUE POOL

Very much hidden away amongst the pine trees is a unique attraction, The Blue Pool. Originally it was a thriving clay mine producing special clay much used by famous porcelain companies: Wedgwood, Minton and Royal Worcester. Today the original deep pit is an intriguing pool of ever-changing colour due to minute clay particles suspended in the water. On the day of my visit the pool was an intense, almost Mediterranean blue. Its lack of oxygen prevents any waterweed growth or existence of fish. The pervading quiet and stillness gives rise to a slightly mystical feeling about the place. On a hot day the smell of the surrounding pine trees is very apparent to the nostrils and flowers and shrubs bloom in profusion. A cream tea and a browse in the well-stocked gift shops after a walk round the pool make a pleasant day's outing; the museum provides the historical background.

My own nostalgic memory of it was at foxglove time when the wood on the left side of the entrance kiosk was a mass of the most beautifully variegated and largest blooms I had ever seen. Resolving to make a shady corner in my own garden into the same little type of glade I acquired the necessary exotic roots but, sadly, to no avail.

The Blue Pool is approached from the Furzebrook Road, signposted on the A351 roundabout south of Wareham. The shops and Tea House are open from April until the end of October.

STUDLAND

Studland is a favourite place, secretive of its beauty and keeping its delights somewhat tucked away. It has four beaches divided by a small jutting headland. The old Tithe Barn has figured on too many sketch books and canvasses to recount. It is close to the beautiful little Norman church built around 1180 and dedicated to St. Nicholas, the patron saint of sailors. Imagination can run riot here and I personally conjure up visions of the many, different infants and the changing fashions that have gathered around the archaic font through the centuries.

The best moment to find tranquillity at this spot is springtime when the church yard and gardens nearby are whispering with nodding daffodils and across a little angel tombstone you can see through the still skeleton trees the wide blue of Poole Bay.

There are four car parks serving the beach, but if you should stop a short while beside the church and tithe barn instead, two things might happen. You might be asked to donate to a collecting box for charity or a particularly friendly robin might perch on your windscreen wiper and take a crumb from your hand as he did from mine.

The walk across Ballard Down to **Swanage** past the promontory of the Foreland is a must. To gaze down upon Old Harry Rock beneath you, if you have a good head for heights, and enjoy his dazzling whiteness at close quarters is very exciting, studded as he is with cormorants and gulls. Pheasants and jays may catch your eye and ear as you walk along the cliff path. Looking westwards the Haystack and Pinnacle rocks are just as impressive with Swanage in the distance.

The strange, gaunt Agglestone, perched high on the heath, is worth a visit. It is a 400-ton chunk of hardened sandstone. Seen from below at dusk the silhouette has a very human aspect. Whilst no confirmation can be found, I think it is safe to assume that Thomas Hardy's poem *By the Runic Stone* has its origins at this spot:

By the Runic Stone
They sat, where the grass sloped down
And chattered, he white-hatted, she in brown,
Pink faced, breeze blown......

Stout footwear is essential for a winter visit to the stone; the twisting path to the heath can be very muddy.

Refreshment at Studland comes in three kinds. On the northeasterly beach (the silver stretch from Sandbanks known as Shell Bay) and at Knoll Car Park there is a cafe and shop, open all the year. Pub lunches are available at the Bankes Arms near the south beach and half way in between, near the middle beach, the lovely old Manor House Hotel also provides food.

SWANAGE

The view of Swanage Bay and 'Old Harry' is at its best from the downs above Peveril Point and these can be reached either by car via the back roads or by climbing up from the Point itself where the lifeboat station, the clock tower and coastguard cottages produce many attractive glimpses en route. Up here I am conscious of the wonderful pink glow that suffuses the sky at times, reminiscent of the lighting on England's east coast that inspired Turner to paint. Swanage air has a special reputation amongst the medical profession for its health giving qualities. Swanage also has the distinction of being mentioned in the Domesday Book.

Some of Swanage's notable features have strange histories; for instance, the gothic clock tower originally came from London Bridge having been erected there as a memorial to the Duke of Wellington. A builder working there who happened to come from Swanage brought it back with him. The same builder rescued the front of the Mercers' Hall in Cheapside, London, during demolition and had it re-erected where it now stands as part of the modern Swanage Town Hall. In this rather spread-out town one of the prettiest corners is the group of old cottages beside the duck pond that is fed by an invisible spring. They are close to the church that is reputed to be older than the castle at Corfe.

Durlston Park, with its strange castle and refreshment room, are only a short run up from the town (up the steep and winding hill past the Peveril Point car parks). The silhouette of this strange building only looks good when seen across the water from the site of the old Tilly Whim Inn (since burnt down). A block of modern flats towers unsympathetically now and almost hides the winding steps half buried in the cliff undergrowth that reward the climber who descends to the idyllic cove below. From the top Durlston Castle seen against the light on a spring morning can look almost elegant.

Having arrived at the Castle, however, the Great Globe of the World made of 40 tons of Portland stone, is a thing to see. It carries strange items of information about the moon, sun and stars and even the flying speed of birds.

But now turning westwards along the cliff-edge path is an exciting experience. Walk past the wind wracked and twisted tamarisk trees and the chart giving a list of sea birds in the vicinity out to the open cliff towards the Tilly Whim Caves and Anvil Point Lighthouse – a lovely and remote part of Dorset. In the breeding season you can get a close view of the nesting gulls.

Swanage is also well known for its Railway. Steam trains run regularly from Swanage past Corfe Castle to Norden where there is a bus connection to Wareham and the main Weymouth to London railway line.

KINGSTON

Perched on the hilltop the tower of St. James Church dominates the first visual impact, the Purbeck stone cottages surrounding it happily.

A visit to the Scott Arms is recommended, covered as it is with Virginia creeper even over the roof – it must be superb in autumn. The view from the beer garden is enchanting and includes an unusual aspect of Corfe Castle in the distance. In this same beer garden there is a tombstone inscribed "Michael Henchard 1807-1852 formerly Mayor of Casterbridge". It was apparently one of the props for the filming of Thomas Hardy's *The Mayor of Casterbridge* in Corfe some time ago and was bequeathed to the pub as a memento and no doubt a reminder of a few lively evenings.

The Scott Arms also boasts a ghost – a lady who, I am told, has a habit of closing doors and is apt to annoy the cleaning ladies sufficiently for them to beseech her to go away, apparently with effect!

The church is delightful, with its unusually cobbled pathway rising steeply up to it (take care here, especially if you are not wearing flat shoes). Built in 1880 it is of cruciform shape and Purbeck stone was used throughout with shafts of Purbeck marble, all quarried and worked here on the Encombe Estate. The timber came from Gloucestershire. Kingston's bells have a wide reputation and teams from many parts come to ring them.

The road leading on to **Langton Matravers** and thus to Swanage provides an exhilarating view of Dorset. The day I drove along exploring the quarries which are passed on either side, the beautiful mellow stacks of Purbeck stone glowed in the sunshine like so many golden nuggets.

Langton Matravers and the neighbouring village of **Worth Matravers** with its ancient church (one of the oldest in Dorset) and cosy inn The Square and Compass, are ideal starting places for walks in the Purbecks and along the Coast Path to Chapman's Pool, Dancing Ledge and St. Aldhelms Head.

KIMMERIDGE

Kimmeridge Bay with its unusual rock formations always provides a fascinating trip. Approaching the bay from the village, past the thatched cottages and Norman church (cream teas are available at the post office), you follow a rather spectacular road, paying your toll as you go – an exciting piece of coastline and country. It is a pleasant spot indeed to which you can descend and park a car on the wide expanse overlooking the sea; perhaps picnicking whilst deciding which way to walk first. To the west you can wander past the old coastguard cottages and up on the cliff. Not very apparent, mercifully, but still visible are signs of progress – the iron donkey, or oil pump, which has chugged away inoffensively for some time now, a reminder that off-shore rigs can spoil the natural beauty of the area. Wild flowers are prolific in this same stretch of path and a half hour's walk produced the specimens included here.

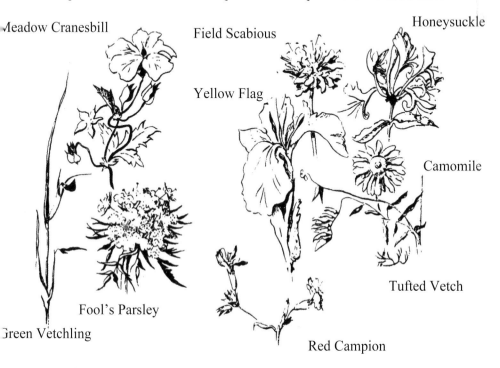

Meadow Cranesbill

Field Scabious

Honeysuckle

Yellow Flag

Camomile

Tufted Vetch

Fool's Parsley

Green Vetchling

Red Campion

Take the path down on the opposite side and you will be close to the old boatshed and strangely ridged beach. Difficult now to think that in years gone by great efforts were made, unsuccessfully, to utilise Kimmeridge shale for making lamp oil and glass at this lonely outpost. It is an unsophisticated corner; here you will find no knick-knack shops or beach cafes but you will probably see fossil hunters in plenty, with their little geological hammers and concentrated gaze. You may decide to have an hour's scramble on the slippery and uneven rocky beach, probing carefully into the fallen cliff fragments to find the remains of Jurrasic ammonites (autocostephanus) that lived when the shale of Kimmeridge was forming itself 145 million years ago. It is believed that ammonites were closely related to the squids of today as they had an array of suckered tentacles surrounding their mouths. Holding one of these ammonites in my hand and looking round the forsaken shoreline on a wild and windy day gave me an eerie sense of unreality.

If you feel full of energy, you can climb the hill and inspect the folly known as the Clavell Tower that was erected by one Reverend John Richards, alias Clavell, of the Smedmore Estate in 1831.

TYNEHAM VILLAGE & WORBARROW BAY

Worbarrow Bay

The proverbial lump appeared in my throat on a bright February morning when I came upon the remote, derelict and yet pathetically beautiful village of Tyneham suddenly. It is peopled now only by ghosts and tourists; its original and unfortunate inhabitants were evacuated in 1943 when the parish was requisitioned.

Despite promises of eventual return any remaining villagers appear to have become total exiles. Today the eyeless sockets of the windows gape from under their moss covered surrounds. The tipsy looking exposed rafters from the cottage roofs which face you as you descend into the valley form a dominant pattern in the sunshine; they caused an upsurge of sorrow and rage within me as I pondered over the folly of war. The sad little turret of the parish church of St. Mary's nearby, now bereft of its bells, could be likened to a body without a heart. The bells, having chimed their last message to the little community before the uprooting, have been removed to join those of St. Michael and All Angels at **Steeple** two miles distant, together with the organ and even some of the original hymnbooks.

In 1977 the Army leased Tyneham Church to be used as a museum and now, at weekends only, the visitor can enjoy its contents and walk once more within the carefully cordoned paths on the Lulworth Ranges including the mile-long trek down to Worbarrow Bay. Notices of 'Danger' and 'Unexploded Bombs' may momentarily chill the spirit but nothing can destroy the beauty of the place where Nature has had a free hand for so long.

Primroses, snowdrops and ferns abound in springtime and in autumn a tangled lace-work of Old Man's Beard covers the barbed wire on the way down to the bay. The church is medieval in origin and close to the gateway stands an oak tree with its attendant notice telling you that it commemorates the coronation of King George V in 1911.

Within the church is a fascinating array of old photographs that tell of Tyneham and Worbarrow life before the storm broke. In these days of mackerel rarity in the bay, particularly interesting is the one showing the beach nearly covered with fat fish from the nets and alongside, looking well pleased with the catch, the men who 'went down to the sea in boats'.

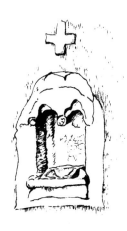

In the oldest part of the church is a 13th century piscina and close by are beautifully illustrated sheets on the wall telling of the off-shore seaweeds, rare plants and animals including the velvet swimming crab, which are able to colonise here; all are protected, of course, from the ravages of humanity by the isolation of the area. So it is indeed 'an ill wind...' after all, as the jovial and helpful Range Wardens will tell you. They are always on duty to watch and to help visitors when the Ranges are marked 'Open'.

Undoubtedly a walker's Mecca, the ups and downs of the countryside, the sea vistas, cliff formations and total peace will tranquillise the most restless of souls. Here in one of God's unspoilt acres walks, carefully timed for you and shown on a leaflet to be found in the church, vary from 1½ to 4½ hours.

There are three car parks within the Range, one at Steeple, one at Whiteway and one at Tyneham itself.

Just one word of warning – the Army reserve the right to close the ranges even at weekends if needs be, so its best to check up before setting out.

THE LULWORTHS

The Doll's House
Lulworth Cove

It is a pleasant road from Poole that bypasses Wareham and continues across the heath to **East Lulworth**. By the roadside, marked by 'Danger, Unexploded Bombs' notices, I saw as a bonus various wild flowers of the rarer kinds. The village is remote and most of the cottages are thatched. The castle, which was erected in 1608, can be glimpsed resting on its hill and artistically framed by the big gates. The castle grounds, which include a chapel, park and animal farm, are open everyday except Saturdays during the summer months. The grounds are closed to the public from 24th December to the beginning of February. On to **West Lulworth**; more thatch and a churchyard apart from its church. You can regale yourself here with a hot pie from the little 'Shop up the Bank' or go to a restaurant if you would prefer.

The big attraction in this area is the **Cove** itself. This is so well known with its restful and circular appearance that I shall not draw it; instead I will turn your attention to the minute cottage known as 'The Dolls House' that is on your right just after you leave the compulsory large car park. Originally it was built by an American as a holiday home but now it belongs to the rest of the estate. It is not an antique but it is intriguing nevertheless.

Hotels, restaurants and ice cream booths here offend the eye but are, I suppose, necessary. The scramble up to the top of the hill on your right as you descend the Cove is well worth the trouble. From here you can gaze down, or go down, to see Stair Hole and look out through a telescope to view Portland Bill across the bay. The Fossil Forest may also be mentioned – more scrambling needed.

Further along this part of the World Heritage Coastline from Lulworth Cove, the famous natural arch of **Durdle Door** should be visited. Perhaps having been to Lulworth first you might then go to the cliff above Durdle Door to watch the sun going down behind it. This is most impressive but preferably go out of season when the caravan park by the approach is silent and the car park empty.

BINDON ABBEY

Just down the Wareham road from **Wool** and almost obscured from sight by the surrounding woods are the remains of the Cistercian Bindon

Abbey, which was restored from its post-Dissolution state two centuries ago. (Much of the stone from the Abbey was used in building Lulworth Castle.) Thomas Weld built the small house and gatehouse here when he interested himself in the Abbey ruins at the end of the 18th century. Today its house and chapel are in parochial use, though permission can be obtained for entry; it is owned by the Weld Estate.

The open coffin of Abbot Richard Maners, which figures in *Tess of the d'Urbervilles*, is easily visible and is shown in the foreground of this Abbey illustration. It will be remembered that Angel laid Tess therein; at the moment of sketching it is full of water!

Just across the fields from the Abbey the magnificent 17th century Woolbridge (Welbridge) Manor stands proudly and next to it the equally famous Elizabethan stone bridge over the River Frome. Here, a picturesque spot so favoured by photographers, you are truly in Hardy Country and can easily leave the present-day world with its tensions and pressures well out of mind.

Along the road between Wool and Bere Regis are two interesting but totally different attractions: **Bovington Tank Museum** and **Monkey World**. They could be combined as a complete Day Out as both provide much to see and do. The Tank Museum houses over 150 of the world's finest armoured fighting vehicles. You can experience the sights and sounds of war and see the various displays of uniforms and military memorabilia as you move through the different galleries. There are occasional Tanks in Action Days that are very popular.

Woolbridge Manor

MONKEY WORLD RESCUE CENTRE

Situated in one of the wildest parts of Dorset this is a unique and beautifully organised and laid out sanctuary for these unfortunate creatures who have been exploited in various parts of the world for nefarious purposes – photographers' props, circuses and, worst of all, laboratories, and from which my favourite little Squirrel Monkeys had been recovered 'just in time'. It is shocking to realise that the lust for money leads, in most cases, to the killing of the mother so that the baby can be smuggled away for exploitation. These primates are, as we are told, our closest relatives and are capable of all the same emotions (look into the eyes of the monkeys on the brochure, you can see it all there), so this Centre, which was set up in 1987, is one of the bright spots in this violent and insensitive world. Their continuing commitment to rescuing abused and ill-treated monkeys means their numbers have grown substantially and the Centre works hard towards rehabilitating them. Inside the 60-acre park they live as they would in the wild, in social groups, in specially designed areas.

Disappointingly it was another cold bleak day that I'd decided to make my visit so most of the inhabitants had left their splendid, open to the sky areas and were indoors in their comfortable and suitably 'furbished' quarters. All of them were busily engaged in 'monkey business' and I was intrigued by the antics of Hebe and Johnny, two youngsters who were being hand reared until they were old enough to join their special group.

The area is so generous that you will have walked a long way by the time you have gone all round (disability facilities are available). One area during the summer is actually a piece of woodland where the monkeys roam free and you are allowed to go in as well provided you do not try to feed or touch them.

Apart from learning about monkeys in their natural habitat there are many energetic activities for children to try here: obstacle courses, mini motorbikes and boating as well as the usual swings and slides.

By now I was nearly frozen but a visit to the café where a hot tea and chocolate biscuit (forget the calories) thawed me out. It is certainly a very worthwhile Day Out.

MORETON

Situated in an unspoilt area of land, Moreton village is the 'Morford' of Hardy's world and the station, which still functions as a wayside halt amidst the woodland, is alluded to in *Fiddler of the Reels*.

The piece de resistance of the district is the church of St. Nicholas that is of a most attractive and unusual shape and which has 12 most beautifully engraved glass windows. These are the work of Lawrence Whistler (brother of the famous Rex) and were completed over a period of 30 years. The original 5 were paid for by War Damage money but the remainder have been provided by private initiative, their theme always being light: candlelight, sunlight, jewel-light, starlight and lastly a spiral galaxy. They are extremely impressive.

Across the road in the picturesque little cemetery is the grave, flower decked and resting beneath the blue cedar tree, of none other than T.E. Lawrence – Lawrence of Arabia, as he was known – who helped to free the Arabs during the First World War. He chose to retire here and bought an isolated, little brick cottage at peaceful **Clouds Hill** nearby as a retreat. The cottage is open to the public during the season on Thursdays to Sundays (inclusive) and is also one of the sites on the Lawrence of Arabia Trail that begins at **Bovington Tank Museum**.

THE RED POST

Daily scores of motorists pass this singular red signpost with its white lettering, situated on the A31 where the road from Winterborne Tomson and Anderson crosses it on route from Wimborne to Bere Regis. It may well pass unnoticed but it has an interesting history. Originally there was a barn building here which used to house the prisoners overnight as they were being walked from Poole to the prison in Dorchester. When I was last in the Priest's House Museum in Wimborne the actual leg irons that they wore during this walk were hanging on the wall. Local legend has it the irons reduced their legs to a red raw state and hence the name 'Red Post'. It was also at this spot that the Town Crier used to announce the holding of the Court Leet nearby at Anderson Manor on St. Martin's Day.

THE PUDDLES

On the main road from Dorchester to Bournemouth you come to the 'Puddle' district and here you should halt awhile and explore. You cannot fail to see **Tolpuddle** of the Martyrs' fame signposted from the main road. It is almost laughable now to think these 6 famous and unfortunate men were sentenced and sent in chains to Australia for 7 years because they had taken an 'illegal oath' to join a Union. In those days this act was considered to be plotting a conspiracy whereas now it almost constitutes the same thing not to join one. If you wish to learn more about the Tolpuddle Martyrs there is a museum (closed on Mondays) dedicated to them in the village.

This attractive village with its thatched cottages, Martyrs' Tree and memorial shelter alongside the main road then continues beyond the bridge and the River Piddle. The road here passes through the pleasant and fertile water meadows with their gently ridged surfaces and tiny bridges used for irrigation purposes, leading you to **Affpuddle**. Here you will find much beauty and interest including the special beach-ends in the church that were carved in 1548 by the vicar.

Exploring further will disclose **Bryant's** and **Turner's Puddles**. Bryantspuddle takes its name from Brian de Turberville who was Lord of the Manor in the time of Edward III.

ATHELHAMPTON

It would be a mistake not to include a visit to the historical and lovely house of Athelhampton. It is really beautiful and has its roots in the Middle Ages. It is reputed to be the site of King Athelstan's palace. Despite all the restorations carried out over the years, it remains medieval with its surrounding courts, walks and walls. The pleasant little River Piddle flowing through the grounds gives added charm.

One of the earliest surviving portions of the house is the 15th century porch that faces you as you approach and has to the right of it a Magnolia Grandiflora believed to be 200 years old. The Great Hall, entered through the porch, has an open timber roof. The original screen inside is no longer there but has been replaced by another originating from an old Devonshire house and which is a pleasure to gaze upon. The Oriel in the Great Hall dates from the reign of Henry VII.

In this fascinating house, so full of interesting corners and objects, you will also be attracted by unusual plant life displayed in appropriate spots throughout. A selection of these is usually for sale in the garden.

Athelhampton boasts of no less than 3 ghosts including a man with no head; a Grey Lady and a Black monk. There are also tales of a pet ape that was walled up in a priest's hole and whose ghost reputedly roams the house. These ghosts may be local colour but in any case as the owner of the house has been heard to say, "It is better to leave them alone", and I think he is right.

Athelhampton is open to the public every day (except Saturdays) during the summer and on Sundays during the winter.

MID DORSET

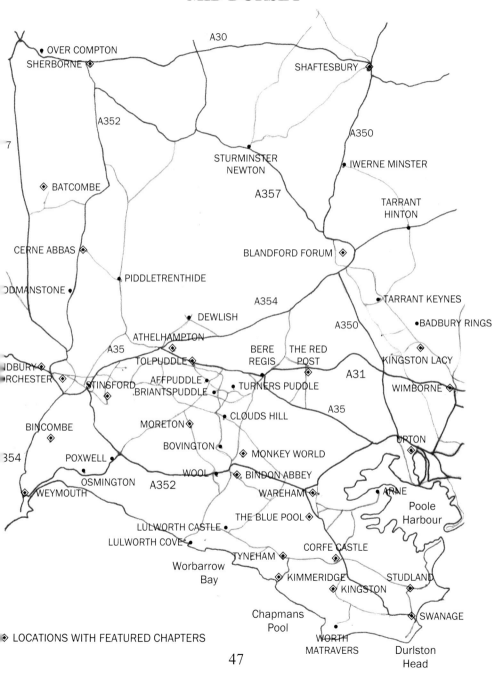

- OVER COMPTON
SHERBORNE ◈

A30

SHAFTESBURY ◈

A352

A350

STURMINSTER
NEWTON

IWERNE MINSTER

A357

TARRANT
HINTON

◈ BATCOMBE

CERNE ABBAS ◈

BLANDFORD FORUM ◈

⦾DMANSTONE •

PIDDLETRENTHIDE

A354

TARRANT KEYNES

DEWLISH

A350

•BADBURY RINGS

ATHELHAMPTON

A35

TOLPUDDLE

BERE
REGIS

THE RED
POST

KINGSTON LACY

A31

AFFPUDDLE

TURNERS PUDDLE

WIMBORNE ◈

⦾DBURY
⦾RCHESTER

STINSFORD

.BRIANTSPUDDLE

A35

BINCOMBE

MORETON ◈

CLOUDS HILL

BOVINGTON

UPTON

354

POXWELL

◈ MONKEY WORLD

OSMINGTON

A352

WOOL

BINDON ABBEY

ARNE

WEYMOUTH

WAREHAM ◈

Poole
Harbour

THE BLUE POOL ◈

LULWORTH CASTLE •

CORFE CASTLE

LULWORTH COVE •

TYNEHAM ◈

Worbarrow
Bay

KIMMERIDGE

KINGSTON

STUDLAND

SWANAGE

Chapmans
Pool

WORTH
MATRAVERS

Durlston
Head

◈ LOCATIONS WITH FEATURED CHAPTERS

47

BLANDFORD FORUM

There is much to be investigated in Blandford with its six-arched bridge over the River Stour, the attraction of its Georgian Town Hall and the fame of its nearby Public School. Amongst various well-known names with local connections is that of Rupert Brooke. Then unknown and in the Navy during the Great War, he was stationed in the Naval Camp for training.

Blandford was a prosperous market town in medieval times but between 1579 and 1731 many fires practically destroyed the town and so it does not have the lure of antiquity to be found in other Dorset towns. However, it was rebuilt in a homogenous style that has an appeal of its own.

The road that leads from Blandford to Sherborne is an attractive drive – winding and with broad vistas. It takes you through several villages, the nicest of which I think is **Sturminster Newton** where Thomas Hardy lived for a while. Here the River Stour is placid and pleasant and spanned by a very fine, arched, medieval bridge.

SHERBORNE

Sherborne is so steeped in history that interested folk should seek out more comprehensive reading than this little guide in which I shall merely remind you that this town and its beautiful golden coloured Hamshill Stone-built Abbey filled with architectural and historical gems, was also the home of Sir Walter Raleigh during his unfortunately short ownership of the Castle and Manor which, since 1617, has been the home of the Digby family. 'Capability Brown' designed the extensive gardens that surround a 50-acre lake, a haunt of many migratory birds. Splendid collections of art, furniture and porcelain are on view at the Castle, which is open from April until the end of October.

About a mile away from Sherborne Castle is the town centre. Cheap Street, its main shopping area, is on a hill. At the lower end of Cheap Street is the well-preserved Conduit where the Cistercian Monks used to wash and shave. It was moved here centuries ago from its original site in the cloister court of the Monastery. Now it is surrounded on Thursday and Saturday mornings with lively market stalls. Nearby are the museum and a passageway through to the Abbey. Sherborne has many quaint corners, much Tudor and Georgian architecture, many antique shops and some famous schools. Altogether it is a subject for a Day Out in itself.

SHAFTESBURY

Standing 700 feet above sea level like an ever-alert sentinel, exposed to every wind, rain or freak weather Nature wishes to bestow, Shaftesbury has much to offer you. Viewing it from below on any side, the mind has no great difficulty in imagining the days when the Abbey stood intact on its heavenly perch where it remained until the Dissolution. Now it is visible only as an enclosed and preserved ruin. All that remains of this important Benedictine community for women (and once the largest in the country) are the excavated foundations of the Abbey church. Its attached museum contains ancient carved stone, Purbeck marble and medieval floor tiles that once adorned the church floor. The bones of St. Edward, king and martyr were unearthed on this site on January 22nd 1931, having lain here in their rough lead box for (reputedly) nearly 400 years, have been removed and now lie in rest in a chapel dedicated to St Edward in Brookwood Cemetery. On display in the museum is the original lead box with a photograph showing the bones. It is worth spending time visiting this corner of Shaftesbury that still retains the peace and quiet that once ruled this site.

Gold Hill
Shaftesbury

In the town centre, Gold Hill with its narrow and rather insignificant little passageway approach from the main street and its extraordinarily steep descent and cobbled surface is spectacular. Beyond, the beautiful landscape reaches into the distance and the steeply angled, assorted cottages are thrown up delightfully against the heavily buttressed retaining wall on the opposite side. This, by the way, is the only remnant of the original Abbey precinct wall. The market scene in *Far from the Madding Crowd* was filmed here.

The building housing the excellent, if somewhat small, museum nearby was once the ancient Doss House attached to the Bowles Arms or 'Sun and Moon', its more usual name. This doss house was used by drovers, jugglers, tramps and similar characters attending the old Shaftesbury Fairs and Markets. Apparently, the pens for sheep and pigs were erected, even at this angle, on Gold Hill itself. Inside the museum I was amused by the wooden, cross-eyed Aunt Sally with its clay-pipe nose and attendant notice of past fairground days 'Break My Nose 1d for three wooden pegs'.

The museum also houses the oldest fire engine in Dorset (1744), a fascinating collection of silk cards given away with cigarettes (does anyone remember the exquisite flowers in silk?), an excellent candlestick and lamp collection and the fascinating 'Byzant'. This was the late medieval emblem that was used with games and dancing on the Sunday after Holy Cross Day at Water Festivals at Enmore Green. A pair of gloves, a calf's head and a gallon of ale were presented to the Lord of the Manor of Gillingham by the Mayor and Burgess of Shaftesbury. This act, in some strange way, retained for them the ancient right to draw water from the springs in Enmore Green. Every drop had to be carried up the slope to the town. Payment for this service was apparently a farthing for the pail if it was carried on the head and two pence for a horse load. I trust you will never grumble about your water rates again! This lofty town has much to offer, with its 94 roads to explore. The oldest part of the town is to the west of Christy's Lane.

LULLINGSTONE SILK FARM
& WORLDWIDE BUTTERFLIES

If you wish to see where the silk for the Queen's wedding dress and more recently for those of Princess Anne and Princess Diana was reared and reeled, go and visit the Lullingstone Silk Farm, now combined with Worldwide Butterflies, in the grounds of the old Manor at Over Compton. This place is a great pleasure. You can watch demonstrations of actual silk reeling on the only machine of its kind in England. You can inspect the piles of strange looking cocoons and silk moths that make them, in all their various stages of life cycle and you can marvel that their silk is, almost unbelievably, three times stronger than steel.

Passion Flower
Butterfly

The silk worm has been domesticated over many centuries and has lost its ability to fly. The larvae are fed 6 times a day on chopped mulberry leaves and after a month or so they spin their cocoon in bunches of straw that are provided. These you can also see. The skeins are twisted into neat hanks and packed in units of 5lbs, each of which is known as a 'book of silk'.

In the breeding display you can wander and observe the wondrous beauty of every conceivable type of moth and butterfly at you ease. Here they flit from flower to flower (real and pseudo filled with nectar) and rest between whiles on the ledges where they can be observed closely. The drawing of the

Passion Flower butterfly from Brazil was done as I knelt beside the glass. Here these gorgeous creatures can fly and breed naturally.

The preserved collection is vast. Particularly interesting is the remarkable camouflage of the Leaf Butterfly from Formosa and Peru; folded on leaves and displayed closely it is almost impossible to discern it from its background. Some have wood grain and others bark camouflage patterns.

The gift shop, of course, is a fascinating place where you can purchase exotic scarves as well as larvae to take away if you are so inclined. I myself had an Indian Moon Moth some years ago. Perhaps a visit to this exciting place will encourage you to grow 'butterfly flowers' and not to be so anti-weed minded when you realise that the humble, yet very attractive, dandelion is butterfly fodder.

THE TOLLERS

Within easy reach of Dorchester are the Tollers, of which my favourite is **Toller Porcorum**, 'Toller of the Pigs' as it used to be in days gone by. A more apt title I feel would be Fred's Toller because apart from the Roman pedestal to the font in the attractive church there is Fred, as delightful an example of topiary as you could find anywhere. It is concocted out of a common thorn bush to which an ivy has devoted itself with much affection. Many visitors, I was told, come year after year to inspect him and enquire after his health. His carer, I believe, is no longer around and Fred is unfortunately looking rather neglected.

When the old vicarage was being renovated and converted into a cottage, building work revealed underground tunnels leading from it to the church and also to the Old Swan Inn across the road. I think it is likely to assume that these were smugglers' secret passages used for concealing contraband.

Toller Fratrum, a few miles away, is supposedly the more attractive of the villages whilst **Toller Whelme** has all but disappeared though it is still mentioned on the map.

BATCOMBE

The little village and church of Batcombe (Hardy's Owlscombe) lie at the base of its hill amid the lovely chalk downs that stretches southwards to Cerne Abbas and Dorchester beyond. The beautiful Blackmore Vale lies to the northeast. In Batcombe Church lies buried John 'Conjuror' Minterne. Legend has it that in the 17th century Squire Minterne jumped his horse from the top of the hill and the horse's hoof knocked down one of the 4 pinnacles on the church tower. The missing pinnacle was apparently replaced early last century. Conjuror Minterne is a strange character in Hardy's *Tess of the d'Urbervilles*.

At the summit of the 800 ft high hill with its magnificent vista over rolling countryside and very much buried in the roadside grass, stands the well-worn stone pillar known as the Cross-in-Hand. You will have to look very carefully to find it and can easily miss it flashing past in a car. It is a remote spot and many different definitions have been given of this strange pillar with its relics of carvings. Hardy uses it in both *Tess of the d'Urbervilles* and *The Lost Pyx*. The Gypsies say it is a wishing stone.

In a delightful tucked-away corner between Batcombe and Sherborne lies **Hermitage**. The place takes its name from the Augustinian Friars who settled here possibly as long ago as the 12th century in what was then the Forest of Blackmore. It is situated in extremely remote countryside which makes for pleasant exploration but make sure you have a full tank of petrol!

The church, dedicated to St. Mary, is called 'The Hermitage' and has a distinctive Queen Anne bellcote topped by a knob.

Not far away from Hermitage, **Hilfield** Church nestles on the side of the hill in its far-stretched parish and makes a particularly interesting visit on account of the beautifully carved 15th century pew ends that are said to have come from Cerne Abbey originally. Don't be surprised to find sheep grazing in this churchyard!

Hunt Scene
Near Dorchester

CERNE ABBAS
AND NEARBY VILLAGES

As you wander up this pleasant valley with colourful willows beside the River Cerne towards the famous giant on the hillside, you will enjoy the chain of villages along the route: **Godmanstone**, for instance, which has the smallest public house in England. It is indeed tiny and was originally a blacksmiths shop. It is reported that when King Charles II stopped here to have his horse shod he asked for a drink and the blacksmith replied, "I have no licence, Sire." So there and then the king granted him one. With its thatched roof and saddle stones outside, it is certainly a quaint corner.

The giant is so well known and much written about that it is hardly worth mentioning him further except, perhaps, for the fact that his powers of fertility, even today, draw childless couples to visit him. What never gets confirmed, of course, is whether his power 'does the trick'!

In Cerne itself it is pleasant to wander down the path alongside the river (off Abbey Street). At the end of Abbey Street in the churchyard, which originally belonged to the Abbey, is an idyllic corner overhung by a magnificent lime tree and under which is situated **St. Augustine's Well**, as it is known. The water sparkles silver as it falls over the kerbstones and behind the ancient pool rises the remnant of an arch. Medieval manuscripts firmly uphold the St. Augustine connection with Cerne and it is said that upon a specific occasion St. Augustine had struck his staff on the ground whereupon the spring appeared.

The road leading from Cerne Abbas to **Piddletrenthide** in the spring is an uplifting experience; on all sides are to be seen quantities of Queen Anne's lace, pink campions and garlic and every now and then you can come across a great sheet of colour from the bluebells.

In the graveyard at Piddletrenthide are to be found two lichen covered tombstones and a notice which says: These headstones mark the graves of William (1646) and Thomas (1616) Dumberfield Members of the family immortalised by Thomas Hardy in *Tess of the d'Urbervilles*.

POUNDBURY VILLAGE

Variety, we are told, is the spice of life and surely nowhere is this more applicable than in Poundbury Village, the project and protégée of the Prince of Wales and his brilliant architects. To wander around the twisting and turning newly formed streets, to a village green containing trees and to absorb the variety of materials used to produce the tasteful design and construction of this little 'kingdom' will not fail to excite you – the architectural contrast to the developers block of 'matchbox' flats that are mushrooming up all over the countryside with increasing regularity, makes the discovery of Poundbury a major spiritual uplift (my reaction anyway). At the time of writing it is still in the process of 'becoming'; phase one having been completed.

So far in Pummery Square there are three shops functioning and a delightful coffee shop. In the handsome Brownsward Hall in the Square there is to be a farmers' market on the first Saturday of each month, which should prove a popular event.

There is a spacious Picture House Gallery where you will find a vast collection of limited edition prints and some originals.

My visit time was limited and it was a bitterly cold day so with my binoculars, sitting in the car I ventured to draw one little corner which attracted me while my friend waited patiently. It was a struggle.

Incidentally, I noticed that the foundation stone had been laid in Prince Charles' presence in 1999. I look forward to seeing phase 2 with pleasant anticipation.

DORCHESTER

Of Thomas Hardy's 'Casterbridge' what can one say? It is so well known, so likeable, so central. It is a glorious town, a delight to enter and explore, and will take much of your time. You may even end up by becoming a member of the Thomas Hardy Society that was formed in 1967. However, apart from its Hardy connections there are many other aspects that may interest you such as its connections with Judge Jeffries. You can investigate the Oak Room at the Antelope Hotel that they say was draped in red for his assize sessions, a result of which 292 people were executed. As you walk up the stairs to this room you can conjure up a few nightmarish visions. You can also visit his lodgings in High West Street, now a restaurant. You may wish to take lighter refreshment, instead, at the café known as 'The Horse with the Red Umbrella'. St. Peters Church with its imposing statue of William Barnes outside is prominent across the road from Judge Jeffries' Lodgings.

Dorchester, from the North

Apart from the Military Museum, dedicated to the honour, service and traditions of the regiments of Devon and Dorset, the delightful Teddy Bear Museum and the Gardens and Walks, there is the very rewarding Dorset County Museum. Here you can view the remains of a Roman coffin found at **Poundbury** and the lectern used by William Barnes for family prayers as well as one of his watercolours, his card case, chess set and his pen. The manuscripts of his poems can be seen and also heard being read in a Dorset dialect by touching a screen.

In the museum there are, of course, portraits and photographs of Thomas Hardy galore and in the facsimile of his study you can see his 3 magnifying glasses and various personal belongings. The item that appealed to me most was his original worn, small worktable and the poem that it had inspired, *The Little Old Table*, which you can read for yourself. The area devoted to Thomas Hardy has been greatly enlarged and enhanced since I first saw it many years ago. (Whilst you are in Dorchester, Max Gate, Hardy's house in Alington Avenue where he lived from 1885 until 1928 can be visited. It was here that he wrote *Tess of the d'Urbervilles, Jude the Obscure, The Mayor of Casterbridge* and much of his poetry.)

Outside the dovecote still remains but, unfortunately, no birds. Perhaps my little drawing of it will encourage the powers that be to replenish the stock. They made a happy backdrop.

From the courtyard you can see the nostalgic sight of an old horse-drawn plough and you can inhale the 'farm yard' air or drink in the atmosphere in the 'Rural Life Gallery', seeing the various implements reminds us that modern housewives have something to be thankful for! An Iron Age clay oven and two fine specimens of mosaic floors from the suite of the Turkish baths excavated at Dewlish Roman Villa are exhibits found within the fine archaeological department. The new Dorchester Gallery gives the fascinating history of Dorchester from prehistoric times to the present day. (The only complete Roman town house in Britain can be seen nearby at Colliton Park. It is located behind County Hall.)

Unexpected items to be found in the museum are two of the earliest paintings of Newfoundland in the world and the gold treasure unearthed from Clandon Barrow and you can see superb ichthyosaurs, ammonites, dinosaur footprints and other fossils from Dorset's World Heritage Coast.

If your appetite for dinosaurs has not been satiated the award-winning Dinosaur Museum in Icen Way is well worth a visit. Open 7 days a week it is very popular with families due to its good mix of actual fossils, life size reconstructions of dinosaurs and hands-on activities and computer displays to inform and entertain.

If you have a penchant for the mysterious, whatever you do don't leave Dorchester without visiting the Tutankhamun Exhibition in West High Street. Venturing in by myself I was amazed by the realistically 'spooky' atmosphere that assailed me. Clutching my sketchbook and making notes needed strong concentration; the evocatively dim lighting and strange artefacts contrived to produce the desired effect, not a little eerie!

So much mystery and theorizing surrounds the young pharaoh as to whom and which parentage he belonged that the enigma will continue through the ages. At only 9 years old his claim to the throne, however, was undoubted as he was of the royal house of Amama and at that early age became Pharaoh of all Egypt. His death, unexpectedly, at only 18 was another mystery and murder was suspected.

I drew what I could, in the difficult circumstances for an artist; the glitter of the gold treasures emerging from the gloom helped. It is an experience not to be missed.

STINSFORD
AND UPPER BOCKHAMPTON

No book on Dorset surely can afford to omit a page on the last resting place of the heart of Thomas Hardy. Portrayed as Mellstock in *Under the Greenwood Tree* Stinsford was a place dear to Hardy and there in the quiet little churchyard his heart lies in the same grave as that of his first wife Emma. As you enter the main gate one of the graves on the extreme left is that of Hardy's father who must receive much credit. After all, had he not made some of the music within Stinsford Church, along with his brother and father in his time? He must also have had much influence on the son who was to unleash upon the world the poems and novels that will never be forgotten.

If that son was still alive today one wonders what he would have thought and how he would have written in the turmoil of the 21st century. Would he have revelled in the new possibilities from a manuscript point of view or would he, like many, have felt like giving up? Whilst his heart lies in Stinsford Churchyard amongst the rest of his family's graves, his ashes lie in Poets' Corner at Westminster Abbey.

Also buried in Stinsford Churchyard is Cecil Day Lewis, former Poet Laureate and father of the oscar-winning actor Daniel Day Lewis. Rumour has it that he was an avid reader and great admirer of Hardy.

If you should happen to travel the stretch of road between Stinsford and Tincleton (Hardy's Stickleford) in May as I did, you will be astonished to see the army of outsized dandelions lined up along the south-facing bank. Their size and colour made it hard to believe they were not chrysanthemums!

Now, probably, you will want to cover the well-worn track to the thatched cottage in the hamlet of **Upper Bockhampton** where Thomas Hardy was born on 2nd June 1840; in its very remote setting the cottage still respeaks his description of it in his earliest known poem *Domicilium*. As one wanders

Thomas Hardy's Birthplace

through the beautiful woods of beech, silver birch and many sweet chestnut trees and come upon a rustic seat halfway along, it is easy to visualise him working on the manuscript of *Far from the Madding Crowd* in these idyllic conditions. To follow the silent winding path uphill and down, crossed perhaps by a fleeting squirrel, until at last his birth place emerges and the scent of orange blossom and stocks can fill the nostrils, helps you to understand so much of his writing. The hamlet of Upper Bockhampton is indeed out of this world, even now.

WEYMOUTH

Continuing along the route from Poole to Weymouth you will pass through **Poxwell**, the Oxwell of Hardy's *The Trumpet Major*, which has a delightful and mellow old Manor House. It has an elegantly shaped gatehouse that will catch your eye from the road as you turn the bend. This manor is the suspected 'Oxwell Hall', the home of Squire Derriman in the Hardy saga.

Further on you cannot fail to see on your right the enormous White Horse on the hillside at **Osmington**, depicting King George III who liked Dorset. The hills in this region contain relics from an earlier age too. **Bincombe** Hill and Bincombe Down were settlements during the Stone and Bronze ages as can be seen by the number of barrows or mounds here. These, however, are known locally as the Music Barrows and are said to belong to the fairy-folk. It is also said that if you put your ear to them at Midday you will hear the fairy orchestra. Bincombe was the site of a military camp during Napoleonic times and from the top of the hill there are commanding views over Weymouth Bay and the Isle of Portland.

From a disappointing entry the town of Weymouth, which can look flat and uninteresting on a grey day, gradually unfolds its cloak of attractions. Here you will find everything, even the good old-fashioned Punch and Judy show and donkeys on the beach. The bathing is excellent along the safe and sandy beach and the Pavilion gives good entertainment including wrestling and dancing. Well-kept gardens and parks and the elegant Floral Clock are noteworthy. Radipole Lake and Lodmoor Country Park complete with its Sea Life Centre, both close to the town centre are also well worth visiting. The model village draws many visitors and is illuminated at dusk in the autumn.

The large shopping area is not very apparent until you walk away from the Promenade and wander down St Alban Street; then you will be delighted at the range of shops and boutiques on offer. The very large statue of George III situated on the Promenade cannot fail to impress. It is inscribed 'George the Third from Grateful Inhabitants on the 50th year of his Reign'. The base of the statue has a lion and a unicorn but gigantic flowering stocks hid them on the day that I did this drawing.

On a completely different wavelength from the rest of the town, however, is the harbour area. Weymouth is an old and busy port and offers regular trips to the Channel Islands. The higgledy-piggledy roofline and varied facades of the houses and chandlers shops and inns are joyous and unmodern. There is always something to watch here; fishing boats, colourful characters mending the trawls, pleasure boats, crane loadings and the chatter of alien tongues. You might even see, as I did, the departure of the schooner brigantine named Christian Bach, built in 1953 in Denmark, just finishing her refit and off for life as a charter vessel in the Caribbean with 7,500 sq. ft. sail area.

Brewers Quay, which requires almost a day itself to explore, is a shopping village and activity complex housed in a sympathetically redeveloped Victorian brewery site near the harbour. Attractions here include The Timewalk, the story of the town's turbulent past and maritime connections complete with authentic sounds and smells! The Weymouth Museum also provides a record of the town's local and social history. Discovery is an interactive science centre with many activities and appeals to all ages of visitors. The gift shop has a unique and interesting array of gadgets, puzzles and scientific toys for sale.

WHITCHURCH CANONICORUM

The day I made my pilgrimage to the shrine of St. Wite in the beautiful church at Whitchurch Canonicorum, the primroses in the lanes bending double and the catkins flying at half-mast in the winters east wind. You, perhaps, would be wiser to visit the shrine on a summer's day.

However, frozen and awed, I knelt and placed my head in turn within the dark apertures of the gaunt stone edifice in the gloomy though highly interesting church interior; the marrow tingles at the thought of the strange heads, limbs and garments that had preceded me through the centuries. The painted inscription beside the shrine tells you that:

Within the upper part is a leaden casket with the inscription in Latin: -
Hic.reqesct.reliqe.sce.wite (here rest the remains of St Wite)

And in the casket are the bones of a woman of about 40 years of age. For centuries this has been a place of pilgrimage, the faithful coming to pray, the sick to be healed. Limbs or garments were placed in the oval openings in the lower part of the shrine. It is not certainly known, but for centuries tradition has it that she was a Saxon woman killed by the Danes on one of the occasions when they landed at Charmouth during the 9th century.

Buried in the churchyard is the famous Bulgarian dissident writer of the 1960s, Georgi Markov, who was murdered in London, supposedly by the Bulgarian secret police, by a poisoned umbrella tip jabbed into his leg. He is buried here because his wife was originally from this village.

You will make another strange discovery in the church with its fine tower and Norman font; you will find that Sir George Sommers, an enterprising Elizabethan who was born in Lyme Regis and who had more than an ordinary penchant for the sea and the adventures that went with it in those days, discovered and gave us the Bermuda Islands, where he died and where his heart was buried. His body was brought back to Dorset. These adventures were then to stimulate Shakespeare to such an extent that he used them as the basis for *The Tempest*.

When eventually I emerged from the gloom into the falling snow I had the feeling that, if St. Wite did not see fit to cure my human ills that morning she might at least bless my endeavours to get this book written.

WEST DORSET

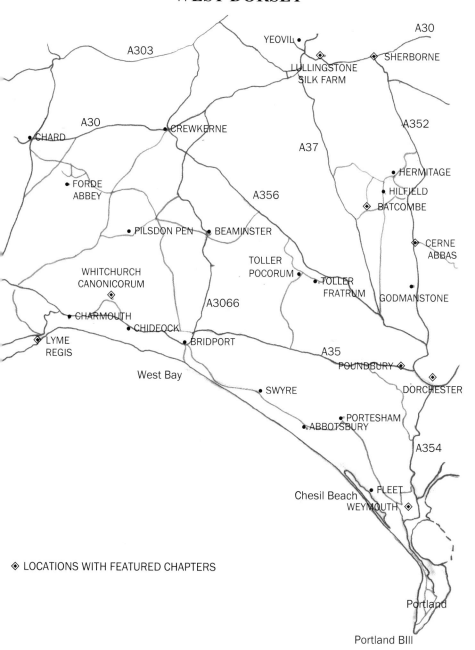

◈ LOCATIONS WITH FEATURED CHAPTERS

LYME REGIS

A unique town this, lying barely inside the borderline between Dorset and Devon, this is the place where the Duke of Monmouth landed. Its main street known as Broad Street, wanders up the hillside from the Square at an extreme angle that undoubtedly will find the weak spots in your leg muscles. If you use either of the lower car parks (one on each side of the Square) it is well to explore this region first. Here you will find the Town Hall with its unique façade, the original door of the old gaol still imbedded and preserved in its outer wall. Just here the River Lym flows into the sea under a bridge consisting of a Norman arch. You will not be aware of the river as you pass over it but if the tide is low inspect it from the beach below (Gun Cliff as it is called) or from a 'peep' a few yards up Coombe Street.

Here at the bottom of Church Street you will find the Lyme Fossil Shop. To me, this alone was worth a visit. In the shop itself there are many tempting fossils in the form of jewellery or ornaments that can be purchased; and the owner who dives and searches for these treasures himself is friendly and informative. The building has been extended to include the cellar below, which is now a well-set-out fossil museum. You will descend by a short, and believed to be old, smugglers' stairway. Here amongst the splendid collection you will find the scattered remains of an ichthyosaurus and also the fascinating fossil sea lily found locally. David Attenborough used some of these specimens for his 'Life on Earth' television programme.

Across the road there is another museum with more fossils and a print of the famous Mary Anning with her hammer; she was the young girl who found the skull, jaw and remains of the ichthyosaurus platyodon fossil reptile in 1811. You can see the original specimen in the Natural History Museum in London.

To view the quaint Cobb you can go either up the main street and fork left at the top that will bring you to a large long-stay car park and then descend by the steep hill alongside; or you can find a short-term park below. There is a birds eye view of the Cobb from the top and whilst you are there it is only a few hundred yards further up to take a look at the much photographed and publicised Umbrella Cottage with its round thatched roof.

Alternatively, starting at the bottom of the hill you can wander along the sheltered Marine Parade to the Cobb past the attractive cottages, hotel and cafes at the foot of the cliff. Here the gentle swish-swish of the small pebbles rising and receding up the beach will lull you into a pleasant stupor. As you near the Cobb you can deviate for a short while and rest in the pleasant Langmoor Gardens situated on the Cliffside, or play crazy golf. At the end of the Cobb itself you can look back at the town and appreciate the layout and, particularly in the evening light, the glory of the distant cliff and hill of Golden Cap.

This area around the Cobb was a particular favourite of Jane Austen and part of her novel *Persuasion* was set in Lyme. In fact this special place with its timeless atmosphere is as popular a holiday resort now as it was a couple of centuries ago.

You can spend an interesting time in the excellent aquarium on the Cobb. As the exhibits are local, the variety and size of the specimens is surprising. In October, so I was told, all the fish are returned to the sea and in the spring the fishermen replenish the stock.

I have visited this aquarium on many occasions but one episode always sticks in my mind: I was sketching one day in the rather dim light when a man carrying a child on his shoulders came in and peered over my shoulder at the scorpion fish, which is anything but attractive, "Coo", he said to the child, "That looks just like your Mum in the early morning!"

It is interesting to find out that John Gould, the great bird lover came from Lyme. Now of course he is world-famous. Humming birds were among his favourites, as his books and collections show. This does not surprise me as I have also spent long, challenging but ecstatic hours drawing and painting these tiny flashing streaks of unbelievable beauty. Wearing a multi-coloured woollen scarf at the time, I was amazed to find that they made efforts to snatch a thread or two for nesting material – totally fearless.

Of the churches, that of St. Michael the Archangel holds the most interest. You will find Mary Anning's grave outside and a memorial to her inside. It was behind this church in the shales at the cliff base that the superb specimen of an ichtyosaurus was discovered in 1978. It had actually retained a lot of skin tissue, mainly around its rib cage.

It is only a few miles further on to Beer, another attractive little coastal town, just across the county border. I received great pleasure sketching the fishing boats from above on the cliff, and enjoying the unusual angle.

THE COAST ROAD FROM LYME REGIS
TO ISLE OF PORTLAND

This road is a truly rewarding stretch, more spectacular on a changeable day than in settled sunshine. Seawards on such a day the sparkling streaks and beautiful cloud shadows across the water set off by the rolling hills on the left and **Chesil Beach** on the right are past description. As you come to the region of Abbotsbury and its famous Swannery, St. Catherine's Chapel perched on the top of a hill dominates the vision. With its four feet thick walls and austere appearance, it causes a momentary shiver – a foreboding looking building, which has stood there for between 400 and 500 years.

Golden Cap
from Lyme Regis

As you approach **Abbotsbury** you will come to a turning on the right at the bottom of the hill marked 'Sub-Tropical Gardens'. I suggest you take it. En route to the Gardens (open all year round) you will notice several old stone seats beside the road which also leads you down to the beach beyond, with its massive and ever changing wall of pebbles which you must climb to view it. The Gardens, a mixture of formal and informal with spectacular woodland valley views, are world famous for their Camellia Groves and Magnolias. Its notable rhododendron and hydrangea collections, rare specimens of tree and exotic plant life add to the attraction and make it awash with colour during the summer.

Back through the village itself you will find merely a single remnant of a wall left of a wall marking the site of the 9th century old Abbey. Nearby, in magnificent shape, is the 276 feet long tithe barn which once stored the wealthy monastic estates produce. Here in the 'Smugglers Barn' you can learn about this area's smuggling past in DVD theatre as told by Isaac Gulliver, Dorset's infamous 18th century smuggler. There is also an indoor play area and children's farm where under 11's can cuddle and feed the animals.

Take time to investigate the rest of the village while you are here with its art galleries, craft centres and interesting shops and tearooms in which to sample the delicious Dorset Cream Teas.

Continue along the road and you will come to the famous Swannery, which is open to visitors from April until the end of October. Originally it was a source of food for the monks but is now a breeding ground and nesting site for nearly 600 Mute Swans.

Heading now for the **Isle of Portland**, you can leave this road and visit **Portesham** and the prominently placed tower that is a monument to Nelson's Hardy on Black Down high above the village. Here you can muse on the Battle of Trafalgar and also enjoy the fantastic surrounding panorama. On a clear day the coastline from Start Point, Devon, beyond Dartmouth to the Isle of Wight is visible.

There are other monuments to be visited on these hills, relics of an ancient age, such as the Stone Age grave on Black Down, known as the Hellstone, the Stone of the Dead.

Then you can press on to the spectacular and fascinating Isle of Portland perhaps taking in Old Fleet Church with its honey coloured stone and leaning gravestones on the way. Nestling beside the lagoon and protected by the Chesil Beach, the tiny village of Fleet was the inspiration for Meade Faulkner's novel *Moonfleet*. A terrible storm in 1824, however, whipped up tremendously powerful waves that washed away the village and part of the church and left a ship marooned on top of the pebble bank.

PORTLAND BILL

Leaving the mainland and crossing the bleak causeway you come to Fortuneswell, which is the capital of the island. As you ascend East Street and New Road you will find at the top a breath-taking view of Chesil Beach and the country beyond; the Portland Heights restaurant and bars, and the vast car park. At its highest point the ground is 496 feet above sea level. Portland houses are strangely assorted and positioned; mostly they are narrow and high but some are very attractive and original old cottages crop up now and again. The road leads on and outward past the huge gaping spaces of the quarries, gaunt in all weathers but having a strange charm. Here and there you will get a glimpse of the sheer drop on the East side to the turbulent and notoriously dangerous waters below. The whirlpool of the Race, the sand trap of the Shambles and the dangers of the magnificent but strange Chesil Beach will be spoken of in tones of fear by the most intrepid of sailors.

Silhouette of
Portland Bill
from the coast road

It has been said in my hearing by an experienced sea-going friend that in his youth there used to be two ways for small boats to approach Portland: one was to take the enormous detour thus avoiding all hazards or the second

71

was to sail so close inshore that you could 'throw a biscuit to the lighthouse keeper'.

Portland's churches are not old but are nevertheless interesting. The prospect of St. George's standing rather in isolation with its unusual architecture, gives one quite a turn – it somehow looks as if it has been wafted here from a land of sunshine and cypress trees and is still unaccustomed to its surroundings.

It was indeed a happy day for the inhabitants of this bleak promontory when Inigo Jones discovered and saw fit to use the now world-famous stone, building with it the Banqueting Room at Whitehall. Thus new life and prosperity began for this isolated world, which in those days was little more than a sheep run. In later years there was still little to attract the tourist: its prison, working quarries, two castles and the lighthouse on the Bill, but now it is a different story. In summer I have seen the stretch of ground leading to the lighthouse covered shamefully, as if under snow, by tourist litter. There was, at that time, a motel and caravan camp just beyond the Museum.

Not the least of the attractions is the old but renovated steam traction engine, which lies beside one of the quarries en route to the lighthouse.

My most recent visit to this place was on returning from a holiday in my favourite Lyme Regis. It was blowing a horrific gale but my more adventurous instincts lured me once more onto the heights to feel and marvel again at the fury and wildness of it all. A hoped-for cup of tea was not forthcoming as the café was closed and I lost a brooch in transit whilst holding onto everything and unable to hear a word of what my companion was saying owing to the wind.

I find the quarries fascinating and even on this occasion the vast one at the top stopped me and I made a quick sketch – it's difficult to depict the enormous drop below.

The incredible Chesil Bank remains the pièce de résistance of this short book. It is nearly 11 miles long, stretching in a mighty and unbroken line from Portland to Abbotsbury and receiving at random, with every tide and storm, yet more pebbles to add to the horde. The strangest thing is Nature's way of sifting these pebbles. The shore being so exposed to the west wind and sheltered from the east and the former being the stronger, it carries by means of the waves aroused the larger ones eastwards and so the largest pebbles are found under the sheltering Portland.

Originally reputed to be the haunt of wreckers and smugglers, this wild stretch yields up many strange creatures such as the blue shark, electric ray, sea devils, sunfish and corals and surprising flotsam from across the

Atlantic. Silver ingots, coins of Constantine and foreign shells have all been found and, in the 18th century, a merman 13 feet long was reported to have been seen.

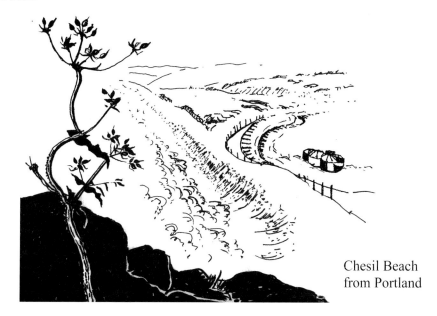

Chesil Beach
from Portland

IN GENERAL

There are various spots still unmentioned or unvisited; for example the beautiful Chapman's Pool – the strange and bewitching cove with the powerful colouring of its cliffs together with the burnt and bleached appearance of the wild undergrowth at their base. There is also the splendid viewpoint from Pilsdon Pen on the B3164 between Broadwindsor and Birdsmoor Gate. Swyre Head and St. Aldhem's Chapel on its bleak foundations should be enjoyed. Bridport is a pleasant enough market town well known for its ancient rope making industry. Nearby, at the fishing port of West Bay, you can watch the glass blowers at work. There are also Chideock and Charmouth through which you pass on the road to Lyme Regis from Dorchester. Both are rather similar in character as they trail picturesquely up the steep hillside. Charmouth has a river and can produce much of historical interest through further probing, as do the prehistoric sites, of which Dorset has many, such as the awesome hill fort of Maiden Castle. Neither should Hambledon Hill, Hodd Hill and Maumbury Rings be forgotten.

Forde Abbey, on the border with Somerset and founded by Cistercian monks over 800 years ago, provides another day out. The Abbey was transformed during the mid 17th century into the magnificent house and glorious gardens you can see today. Other Dorset gardens open to the public and well worth a visit include Kingston Maurward Gardens and Animal Park near Dorchester and Mapperton Gardens at Beaminster.

Beaminster itself, a historic small town built in the local orange limestone, has much to offer and a visit should certainly be made to the series of eight attractive Tarrant villages following the course of their namesake river.

Cormorants in Poole Harbour

Walkers have so much to choose from, apart from pretty villages and quaint country pubs to visit, there are miles of paths along this world-famous coastline with spectacular views. From the Downs of West Dorset to Cranborne Chase in the northeast of the county, not forgetting the beautiful Blackmoor Vale, there are large unspoilt areas of countryside to explore. Many sites such as at Arne, a large nature reserve overlooking Poole Harbour that can be reached by road from Wareham across open heath land, provide excellent bird watching opportunities. You may even glimpse the elusive Dartford Warbler. Various Dorset Country Parks boast nature trails and have other attractions, too.

There are more Family Parks and museums with collections as diverse as toys, clocks, cider, electrical appliances, and costume to be visited. Indeed, going to the Bournemouth International Airport at Hurn, which is where the Dorset Aviation Museum is situated, combined with a trip to the nearby Alice in Wonderland Family Park would make an ideal family **Day Out In Dorset**.

CONCLUSION

By a strange coincidence I am once again concluding this little book when the gardens and hedgerows are lit up by blossoming cherry trees and daffodils and courageous butterflies are venturing out from hibernation and the birds are busy with nesting matters. I have done more exploring, discovering and eliminating, my eyes and hands are not quite as good companions as they used to be and by the time this book reaches the bookshops I shall be 89 – a long way to look back. This was very much brought home to me yesterday by the announcement of the passing of the universally loved and gracious lady, the Queen Mother, bringing with it the end of an era that has also been mine. As I see it her life at the age of 101 has been as outstanding as the Dorset coastline; enduring all the storms and challenges thrown up by this ever-changing and turbulent world, whilst still having managed to give pleasure and enjoyment to so many people. She will leave an irreplaceable gap.

However, life goes on and today I heard that satisfying noise – the drone of a bumble bee. I was also enchanted by the elegance of the cascades of delicate catkins, wine coloured twigs and the strong contrast in the black and white trunks of the silver birch trees. As an artist whose work has been mainly inspired by the natural world and growth around me (even the so-called 'weed' the dandelion which, by the way, is butterfly food) the old saying that the best things in life are free still holds good for me. So in your roamings don't disregard the structure and beauty of nature's 'tinies'. At the risk of horrifying the gardening world I'm enclosing my poem – just another point of view!

It is now Easter and that special 'something' is in the air; a feeling of pleasant anticipation of holiday time ahead and I'm hoping my memories and reactions from my own expeditions will get you planning many happy **Days Out in Dorset**.

An Artist's Ode to a Thistle

Oh, thistledown, thistledown
Whither away?
Where will you bloom
On next summer's day?

Will you go far
Or will you go high,
Or keep close to the ground
As gently as you fly?

Your mark you might make
In flower-bed soil,
And its symmetry neat
Folk think you would spoil.

But if in a hedgerow
A lane or a field,
At liberty there
Your glory to yield.

Or lighten the way
Of motorway driving,
Up fume-laden banks
To be manfully striving!

The gardeners don't like you
But thistledown, dear,
I am utterly happy
Whenever you're near.

I will leave you to mellow
And depart as you may
And hope we will meet
On another year's day!

WEB SITES

Alice in Wonderland Family Park, Hurn
www.aliceinwonderlandpark.co.uk

Abbotsbury – Swannery, Tropical Gardens and village attractions
www.abbotsbury-tourism.co.uk

Athelhampton House and Gardens
www.athelhampton.co.uk

Blandford Tourism
www.ruraldorset.com

Blue Pool, Wareham
www.bluepooluk.com

Bournemouth Aviation Museum
www.aviation-museum.co.uk

Bournemouth Oceanarium
www.oceanarium.co.uk

Bournemouth Tourism
www.bournemouth.co.uk

Bovington Tank Museum
www.tankmuseum.co.uk

Brewers Quay, Weymouth
www.brewers-quay.co.uk

Christchurch Tourism
www.christchurch.gov.uk

Compton Acres, Poole
www.comptonacres.co.uk

Deep Sea Adventure, Weymouth
www.deepsea-adventure.co.uk

Dinosaurland Fossil Museum, Lyme Regis
www.dinosaurland.co.uk

Dinosaur Museum, Dorchester
www.dinosaur-museum.org.uk

Discovery, Weymouth
www.discoverdiscovery.co.uk

Dorchester Tourism
www.westdorset.com

Dorset County Museum, Dorchester
www.dorsetcountymuseum.co.uk

Dorset and East Devon Heritage Coast
www.jurassiccoast.com

Forde Abbey
www.fordeabbey.co.uk

Highcliffe Castle
www.highcliffecastle.co.uk

Keep Military Museum, Dorchester
www.keepmilitarymuseum.org

Knoll Gardens, Wimborne
www.knollgardens.co.uk

Larmer Tree Gardens
www.rushmore-estate.co.uk

Lulworth Castle Park
www.lulworth.com

Lyme Regis Tourism
www.lymeregistourism.co.uk

Mapperton Gardens, Bearminster
www.mapperton.com

Monkey World, Wareham
www.monkeyworld.org.uk

Moors Valley Country Park
www.moors-valley.co.uk

National Trust
www.nationaltrust.org.uk

Natula (Publications) Ltd
www.natula.co.uk

Poole Pottery
www.poolepottery.co.uk

Poole Tourism
www.pooletourism.com

Russell Cotes Art Gallery & Museum
www.russell-cotes.bournemouth.gov.uk

Shaftesbury Tourism
www.ruraldorset.com

Sherborne Abbey
www.sherborneabbey.org.uk

Sherborne Castle
www.sherbornecastle.com

Sherborne Tourism
www.sherbornetown.co.uk

Splashdown, Tower Park, Poole
www.splashdownpoole.co.uk

Swanage Railway
www.swanagerailway.co.uk

Swanage Tourism
www.swanage.gov.uk

Teddy Bear Museum, Dorchester
www.teddybearmuseum.co.uk

Tolpuddle Martyrs Museum
www.tolpuddlemartyrs.org.uk

Tutankhamun Exhibition, Dorchester
www.tutankhamun-exhibition.co.uk

Walford Mill Craft Centre
www.walford-mill.co.uk

Wareham Tourism
www.purbeck.gov.uk

Weymouth Tourism
www.weymouth.gov.uk

Wimborne Minster
www.wimborneminster.org.uk

Wimborne Model Town
www.wimborne-modeltown.com

Wimborne Tourism
www.visiteastdorset.com

INDEX

INDEX (cont)